Recipes from
an Old Farmhouse

LSS
Cookery

RECIPES FROM AN
OLD FARMHOUSE

Alison Uttley

Illustrated by Pauline Baynes

FABER & FABER
3 Queen Square London

First published in 1966 by
Faber and Faber Ltd
3 Queen Square London WC1
Second impression December 1966
First published in this edition 1973
Printed in Great Britain by
Latimer Trend & Co. Ltd., Whitstable
All rights reserved

ISBN 0 571 10178 X

Contents

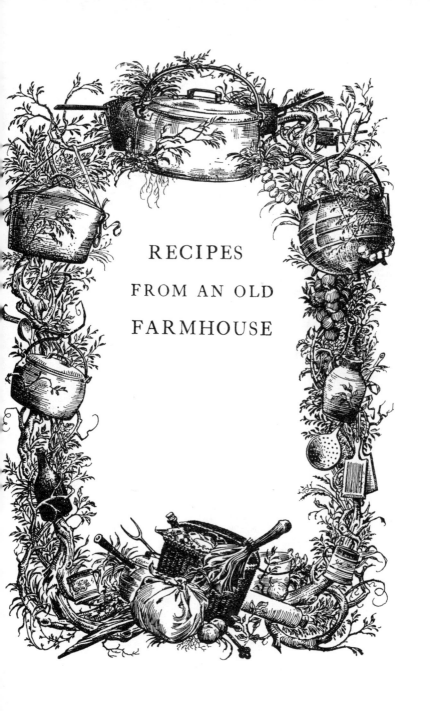

RECIPES

FROM AN OLD

FARMHOUSE

COOKERY in our old farmhouse was an important part of life, and I was a wide-eyed witness of baking and brewing, of boiling and stewing, as I played with a doll or sat on a stool close to the big table, and watched while I waited to scrape the big yellow bowls with a little tea-spoon to get the fragments left. Children were eager tasters; we had the curly crust which dropped from the edge of the crisp loaves of newly baked bread, kissing crust, and we had small turnovers and twists of pastry baked especially for us, for a dolls' tea party.

So cooking was a time of happiness for us, as we dipped and tasted and smelled the good odours, but for my mother and the maid it was hard work. Everything was cooked in the oven or on the stove. The fire was made up to a roaring furnace, to get the oven hot, a beautiful fire in winter but a trial in summer, when it blazed just the same.

The cooking was done on a large scale. Enormous baking tins were used, large joints were roasted, and large cakes were made, also dozens of little ones. We were lavish with food, but nothing was wasted, and poor people were fed with left-overs. When we went to visit friends we took a well-stocked basket with cakes and jam and dainties, with potted meat and bottles of cream, for there was often somebody ill.

We lived far from the simple village shops, and we had sudden calls for meals from people who visited us unexpectedly, so there always had to be a good supply of food in the house. On the day I brought about fifty children home from school to have tea a feast was made, for eggs, butter, milk and cream were always available, and buns and cakes filled the tins. We had food to give away to the beggar and the wanderer, the travelling tinker and the odd journeyman and dealer. Nobody who came so far could be refused, and even the gypsy with her basket of clothes-pegs and the pedlar with his tinware were regaled with a piece of cake and a cup of tea to cheer them on their hungry way. There was poverty, and we were reminded of this every day.

My mother cooked without a cookery book, but some of her recipes were written in her thin delicate sloping handwriting in a book I now possess. The recipes vary from cakes and meat to cough mixtures and syrups, and drinks for the hayfield and for the horse. There are several pages written in my own childish handwriting, set out neatly as if it were a school exercise, underlined with red ink. I copied out recipes given to my mother by country people, and these are indexed in red ink and stiffly written.

At the end of the book are the notes of joints of pork sold to the people in the village, the squire, the clergyman, the draper and ironmonger and the retired governess of the Castle. The weights and prices are there, an extra source of income, from the killing of one or two pigs in late autumn.

Loin of pork is 7d. a pound, bacon is 8d., ham is 10d. and spare-rib is 2d. Rich and poor bought the pork, which was excellent. We cured the bacon ourselves and cured the hams. They lay on the stone benches in the dairy, with salt rubbed into them, and the brine dripped down through holes in the bench to vessels below. The drip, drip frightened me as I went there at night with a candle.

Our cooking utensils were very old-fashioned even for those days of the late nineteenth century. They had been in the house for a hundred years, mended perhaps but still good. We never bought a saucepan, but used the old brass saucepans of my grandmother's time. They were treated carefully, scoured with fine sand, and wiped dry before they went on a shelf in the kitchen. Two of the pans were like top hats, deep and narrow, and they fitted into the long hole over the fire. They were made of blocked tin, very thick and strong. The frying pan was enormous, and it was seldom used except on pancake day. The bread board and the rolling pin too were of vast size, smooth as glass, and white as snow. The baking tins were extra large, but we had one or two small tins and a Dutch oven made by the village tinsmith to our order. Patty pans were of many sizes, some large, some small, some fluted and some plain. Dozens of these old thick little pans were stacked on the dairy shelf, with the tins for gingerbread men.

On the shelf in the brewhouse were iron saucepans of varying sizes, in order, beginning with a monster pan to hold a ham, and decreasing to one about a pint in size. They were clean and dry, and smooth.

I had some cookery lessons at school, and I was charmed by the small rolling pins and the pretty dusters and cloths and little bright tins we used. Water came out of a tap in the wall, unlike our water troughs, and much quicker to use.

Some of our recipes were named after the towns or villages, and one of the most famous is Bakewell Tart. I went to school in this small market town and my father used to visit the well-known market for cattle, held on Monday mornings, when cows were driven across the narrow medieval bridge, scaring us so that we had to take refuge in the triangular niches in the bridge. There we stood, as the poor cows were hurried along by shouting drovers, and we saw the startled eyes looking at us. I was filled with sorrow for them, we always treated cows with care.

Bakewell Tart

(The local name was Bakewell Pudding, for the tart was really for the pudding stage of a meal and not for tea.) Cover a wide shallow dish with thin puff paste. Put in it a layer of jam, preferably raspberry, but any kind will do. It should be about half an inch thick. Take the yolks of eight eggs and the beaten whites of two. Add half a pound of melted butter and half a pound each of sugar and ground bitter almonds. Mix all well together, and pour into the pastry case over the jam. Bake for half an hour, and serve nearly cold.

This was one of our favourite dishes, but it was a rich dish for special occasions only. Eggs were plentiful and cheap, and we used them lavishly, except in winter when the price rose. In summer they were twenty to the shilling, large new-laid eggs.

In the winter, as a variant from porridge we had Frumenty, or Flummery as it was sometimes called. This was a dish of whole wheat ears, with the husks blown away.

They were put in a big earthenware covered bowl, like a casserole, and covered with water. They stayed in the warm oven about three days. They became soft and jellied and delicious. We ate this with new hot milk and sugar on top. The process of slow cooking was called 'creeing', when applied to wheat or barley or any corn. This is the old word, from the French *crever*, now forgotten except in country places.

Spanish Flummery

Dissolve two ounces of gelatine in a quart of water. Add the rind of a lemon and the juice of two. Add sugar to taste and half a pint of sherry. Then add the yolks of six eggs well beaten. Put this to boil on the fire a short time. Strain it and when cold pour into a copper mould.

This exotic recipe I think we never tried out.

THOR CAKE

&

GINGER-
BREAD

DERBYSHIRE Thor cake (or Thar cake as some people called it), was baked and eaten in the autumn for Guy Fawkes Day, and for the country Wakes Week when the swings and roundabouts came to the villages to remind us of merriment and joy. It was a cake for the mid-morning, and slices were cut and spread with butter and eaten as we ran about the fields, with a mug of milk for a sip now and then. Here is the recipe.

Thor Cake

A pound of medium oatmeal and half a pound of good fresh butter, half a pound of Demerara sugar, and four ounces of black treacle, half an ounce of ground ginger and a pinch of salt, mace and nutmeg, one egg, four ounces of sliced mixed candied peel. The dry ingredients were mixed and the butter warmed and hot treacle added. All the ingredients were kneaded together like bread, turned out on a pastry board and rolled out in a piece about two inches thick. This was baked in a large greased and lined meat tin, for about three quarters of an hour, until the cake was

done. Slices were cut off as needed when the cake was cold.
For tea it was eaten with butter.

This cake used to be our food on Guy Fawkes night
when we ate it under the stars, with mugs of hot milk, or
spiced elderberry wine for adults. We watched the sparks
fly, we shouted at the fireworks as we had our feast.

Thor Cake, as made in a Carsington farmhouse

A pound of fine oatmeal and a pound of flour are mixed
and three quarters of a pound of butter rubbed into the
mixture. Add a pound of Demerara sugar, a pound of
treacle warmed, two ounces of candied peel coarsely cut,
two teaspoonfuls of baking powder, a teaspoonful of
ground ginger and a pinch of salt. Knead well and roll out
fairly thin. Cut into rounds and bake in a moderate oven.

This differs from our own Thor cake, as we kept it
thick, and did not cut it into rounds. The traditional Thor
cake was much heavier, a farm cake for toilers in the
fields, perhaps.

Gingerbread

Flour two pounds and medium oatmeal a quarter of a
pound, half a pound of butter, half a pound of Demerara
sugar, treacle one pound, two eggs, an ounce of ground
ginger, two ounces of candied lemon peel, a teaspoonful
of bicarbonate of soda, and a little milk. Mix to a thick
paste, adding the soda, dissolved in warm milk, last.
Pour in a buttered and lined baking tin. Bake for an hour
or more.

Travellers' Gingerbread

This was more delicate and less solid. Half a pound of
butter and a pound and a half of flour, half a pound of

treacle and half a pound of brown sugar, two eggs, half an ounce of ginger and a teaspoonful of bicarbonate of soda. Add nutmeg and candied peel, and mix with rose-water. Rub the butter in the flour, add all the other ingredients except the bicarbonate of soda which must be added last dissolved in milk. Make into a stiff paste with rose-water. Roll out in little balls. Mark with finger and bake in a flat tin.

Another Gingerbread

Take one pound of flour, and rub into it a quarter of a pound of melted butter, and a quarter of a pound of best lard. Add half a pound of sugar, half an ounce of ground ginger, a pinch of nutmeg and some lemon candied peel. Mix to a stiff paste with two eggs. A teaspoonful of bicarbonate of soda dissolved in warm milk is added last and the mixture is poured in a baking tin and baked.

Yorkshire Parkin

Mix a quarter of a pound of flour, three quarters of a pound of oatmeal and half a pound of treacle together. Work in two ounces of lard, a teaspoonful of ginger and two teaspoonfuls of baking powder. Bake in a slow oven in a flat tin.

Another parkin recipe is called Mrs. Lowe's Parkin. I think Mrs. Lowe was one of my mother's friends, who used to visit us in winter, wearing a black satin apron. Cakes were often called after the donor of the recipe.

Mrs. Lowe's Parkin

Mrs. Lowe took two pounds of fine oatmeal, and half a pound of flour, half a pound of butter and half a pound of brown sugar. The fat was worked into the flour and the oatmeal, and the sugar added. Then a pound and a half altogether of syrup and treacle warmed was poured into the mixture, and two ounces of candied peel, the grated rind of a lemon and two ounces of ground ginger added. Lastly came a teaspoonful of baking powder, and a little hot water to mix. It was baked for an hour and a half in a not too hot oven. Then cooled and cut in wedges.

There was of course no self-raising flour, and even when it came into use we never had it. We bought flour by the great sack, which was lifted by a man to the dairy bench, and there it stood in the corner, a weight of flour with a heavy tin flour scoop by its side and the rolling pin and the large old wooden pastry board. The sack was kept closed lest a wandering mouse should discover it.

Mrs. Lowe was the origin of another cake, and as the recipe follows the parkin recipe in my mother's cookery book it must have dated from the same visit, when I was a tiny child. It is more luxurious, a best cake.

Mrs. Lowe's Cake

One and a half pounds of self-raising flour is used and this to me shows that Mrs. Lowe came from a town, as we did not have anything self-raising. Half a pound of butter is added, and mixed to a crumb. Then add one and a half pounds of sultanas and a quarter of a pound of candied peel. Mix with three eggs and a little milk. Put in the oven. Take six ounces of almonds, blanch and split them. Add six ounces of fine sugar, and then add some almond essence. Mix with an egg. If too wet add a little flour. When the cake is baked put the almond mixture on the top and brown in the oven. For icing the cake, mix six ounces of icing sugar with a little hot water and pour on the cake, drying it before the fire.

Whole-wheat meal Gingerbread

A pound of whole-wheat meal is required. (It was ground in the village from local wheat.) Melt six ounces of good beef dripping, from sirloin if possible. Add one pound of treacle to the hot fat. Now rub three teaspoonfuls of ginger, ground, and five ounces of brown sugar into the wheat meal. Then add the melted dripping and the treacle which must be well mixed. Lastly add a teaspoonful of bicarbonate of soda which has been dissolved in one and a half gills of milk. Spread on a well-greased deep baking tin, and bake. Cut into squares as soon as it is done.

(Four gills made a pint in our society.)

Gingerbread Fingers

Mix four pounds of flour with twenty ounces of butter, and two pounds of golden syrup. Add two ounces of ground ginger, and two pounds of sugar. Roll out very thin, and cut into long sticks. A few minutes in a hot oven will bake them crisp.

This must have been a recipe for a party of shooters, or for haymakers or a school treat, by the quantity. Sometimes we had twenty or more to feed.

Gingerbread men were made and sold in country places at Easter Fairs and Autumn Wakes week, and they are still fashioned in old moulds, for some were exhibited recently at the London Meeting of Women's Institutes. I have one of the prints for making these little figures, but mine dates back to the time of the Napoleonic Wars. It is a solid block of beech wood, close-grained and hard, with seven designs cut and carved with intricate and delicate accuracy, four on one side and three on the other.

There is a farmer with his sheaf of corn and a sickle, an admiral with a shock of hair and a tricorne hat, a marine with a sword, a little church with three windows and a tower, a bird on a tree, a basket of fruit and a sportsman.

These figures were filled with a sweet gingerbread mixture of fine quality, pressed very close to the mould. Then the shapes were removed carefully and baked in a flat tin. Sometimes we placed thin pastry coated with sugar in the moulds, and then removed, trimmed and baked it.

In my childhood we had small moulds of heavy blocked tin, with designs of a horse, a tree, a leaf, and a man. I discovered these on the high top shelf of the dairy, put away by former generations, and forgotten. Life was a continual discovery of lost treasures. On baking day we were allowed to bake little pastry men with currant eyes, and gingerbread animals and men from the fine gingerbread paste.

The gingerbread men at the fairs were not gilded as in Elizabethan days, but they had coloured hats and scarlet buttons on their coats or white buttons of sugar. Ashbourne was a town for these little men.

Gingerbread Wafers

These wafers, the recipe says, are thin for gingerbread men and such toys. Half a pound of butter is rubbed into half a pound of flour. Half a pound of white sugar and a little powdered ginger are added. Put four tablespoonfuls of cream into a quarter of a pound of golden syrup and then mix all together for five minutes. Drop in teaspoonfuls on a baking tin, and bake in a hot oven, or make into paste for the gingerbread moulds.

This recipe came from an ancient village where we drove to have tea at the Inn where our friends lived. Horses and people and the noise of the fair and market day are mingled with this gingerbread.

PUDDINGS

For the height of summer the well-known cold sweet, Summer Pudding, was made from any fruit that was ripe. So we had it made from red currants when the red berries were translucent, gleaming by the garden wall, of black currants when the strings of black juicy berries covered the trees by the white rose, or of raspberries. The best loved was the summer pudding made from the wild bilberries growing in Bilberry Wood on the top of a hill. We set off on a summer afternoon with little tin cans and a basket containing a bottle of milk, and china mugs, and cakes for a picnic tea.

Bilberry Wood was an enchanted place. There lived a fox and rabbits, many birds and lovely trees. The mountain ash and silver birch added to the lightness of the air. There were no dense frightening places in this wood. All was light and air, so heather grew in the sunny spaces and bilberry bushes made little round springy cushions where we sat for tea. When the berries were ripe we sat on the projecting black stones and picked the blue-black berries which we threaded on stalks of fine grass. We came home

27

with blue-black mouths and fingers, for we ate nearly as much as we gathered. The bilberries growing in that wood, and in the lane under the dark walls, were so fresh that each had a bloom on its skin, and we picked the fruit trying not to harm this delicate painting by nature. The bloom on fruit always interested us, and we were careful with the Victoria plums, the damsons and the apples, regarding the bloom as something mysterious, like lace on a dress, or a feather on a bird, a decoration not made by man.

Summer Pudding

The fruit is simmered with sugar until soft. Then a basin is lined closely with strips of bread. The pieces must make a close-knit mould inside the bowl, with no cracks. Into this pour the hot fruit and enough of the juice to keep the fruit fairly stiff and to saturate the bread. Cover the top with a lid of bread, using no crusts. Finally place a saucer on the top with a heavy weight—two or three pounds. Leave the pudding all night in a cold place, for the juice to permeate the bread, and the whole pudding to congeal to firmness. The next day carefully turn it out and serve with thick cream or egg custard.

Chocolate Pudding

Cream three ounces of butter and four ounces of sugar together. Stir into this the yolks of two eggs and six ounces of bread-crumbs. Melt a quarter of a pound of chocolate in a quarter of a pint of milk and add to the mixture. Add vanilla to flavour. Beat the two whites of the eggs to a froth, and add lightly. Pour into a buttered mould and steam for one hour.

Queen of Puddings

Boil half a pint of milk with an ounce of butter. Pour it over half a pint of bread-crumbs, and add the grated rind of a lemon, the yolks of two eggs, and two ounces of sugar. Pour into a well-buttered pie-dish and bake until set, about twenty minutes. Beat up the whites of the eggs to a stiff froth. Spread jam over the pudding and pile the whites of egg on top. Sprinkle with sugar and let it colour pale brown in the oven.

This was our birthday pudding, and a welcome pudding for friends, or as a treat for a child.

Leicester Pudding

To two cups of flour, add a quarter of a pound of chopped suet, half a pound of currants, a tablespoonful of sugar, and half a pint of milk. Mix a teaspoonful of bicarbonate of soda with some of the milk and add last. Steam for three hours.

Canary Pudding

This was an amusing game of weighing, with eggs as weights.

Cream the weight of three eggs in butter with the weight of three eggs in sugar. Add the three eggs and the weight of two eggs in flour, with the grated rind of a lemon. Boil in a mould for two hours and serve with white sauce.

This yellow pudding was enjoyed by children who thought it had a particular link with the yellow canary who sang in the cage above the kitchen table. A name makes a vast difference to a child's mind, and a pudding called after a pet canary was in demand.

Caramel Pudding

Take two ounces of loaf sugar and two tablespoonfuls of cold water and boil together until a nice brown colour. Pour into six little tins or moulds and let it run round the interiors to coat all places. Take half a pint of milk or cream, cream if possible, and two egg yolks (but if milk use three yolks and one white), a little vanilla and sugar. Heat the milk, or cream, and add it to the eggs well beaten and sweetened. Pour it into the little tins and steam fifteen minutes or until set. When set turn out on a dish. These are good hot or cold.

Orange Sponge

Put half an ounce of finest leaf gelatine in a pan with half a pint of hot water and the rind of two oranges. Stir until the gelatine is dissolved. Strain into a basin and add the juice of the oranges. Cool it. Put in it the raw white of an egg and whisk until stiff. Heap on a glass dish, or put into a wet mould. Do not whip too stiffly if a mould is used.

Junket

We used junkets very often, and we never tired of them. Creamy milk fresh and warm from the Jersey cow was brought into the house for junkets. It was poured in a glass dish and a little sugar added and a drop of vanilla essence. Then a large teaspoonful of rennet to a pint of milk was stirred in and the milk left to set. A little nutmeg was grated over the surface as soon as the junket was ready.

Sometimes we had individual junkets, the original junket being mixed in a jug and then poured into glasses. When set, thick cream topped each glass.

French Pancakes

Cream two ounces of butter with two ounces of fine sugar and beat in two eggs. Stir in lightly two ounces of flour and add half a pint of warm milk. The milk will slightly curdle the eggs. Beat again, then cover with a cloth and leave the batter to swell for an hour. Butter half a dozen tea saucers and pour some of the batter in each. Place in a hot oven until cooked. This is a delicate matter and the oven door must be opened now and then to see that the pancakes are not cooking too fast. Remove from the oven when pale brown and place a dessertspoonful of raspberry or strawberry jam on top of half the pancakes. Cover these with the remaining pancakes. Roll into half-moons. Serve on a warm dish, and sprinkle the outsides with sugar.

This was a popular and easy dish, which we all enjoyed. The saucers interested me, for we often had beautiful old saucers from a long-ago broken set of china, which we kept for this pudding as they were large and old-fashioned. I liked to cook in a saucer, which was more attractive than an enormous piece of tinware.

Six Cup Pudding

This was a pudding with a simple recipe which was easy to remember, for everything was measured with a cup. We had a cupful of flour, of sugar, of currants and of raisins, a cupful of butter and one of milk and a beaten egg mixed. All these cupfuls were well mixed together with a teaspoonful of baking powder, and the resultant mixture was steamed for two hours. It was eaten with egg custard.

Another common pudding was 'Spotted Dick'. The name was important to us, it was a joke, and Dick was meant to be a Dalmatian dog or a piebald pony.

Spotted Dick

The pudding was a mixture of a cupful of flour and a cupful of suet, a cupful of currants, an egg and a little milk to mix. It was a boiled dumpling pudding for a working day, to appease the hunger of farm men, a primitive pudding known through the centuries, boiled in a cloth.

An old-fashioned Derbyshire pudding

A batter pudding is made in the usual manner, with four ounces of sieved flour and a pinch of salt put in a bowl, and a well formed in the centre. Into this drop two eggs. Beat in the flour, allowing it to fall from the sides until the eggs and flour are made into a batter. Add slowly half a pint of milk, and a tablespoonful of cold water, beating all the time to get rid of lumps. Keep beating until the batter is so light that some bubbles form. Cover with a cloth and leave an hour for the flour to swell. Have ready a pound of gooseberries, picked and washed and fresh. Place a little dripping in a deep meat tin, and make it hot in the oven. Pour in the batter when ready and drop the gooseberries with a little sugar dredged over them into the batter, keeping the fruit separately spaced. Put the tin in the oven and bake for one hour. This pudding is served with sugar, and the sour taste of the gooseberries mingles well with the smooth taste of the batter. It was a cottage pudding, much loved for the ease in cooking it.

On very busy days, such as wash-day when owing to bad weather a lot of washing had accumulated and everyone was too busy to cook, we had a special pudding, called by the title I liked so much, Hasty Pudding. It was made in five minutes, a simple dish, despised by adults but adored by children, partly for its romantic name, and because we saw it boiling with haste to be ready.

Hasty Pudding

Flour was mixed with cold water to a thick batter. Then spoonfuls were dropped into a large pan of fast-boiling salted water. The flour formed queer shapes, and these shapes were taken from the pan with a large perforated ladle and dropped on hot plates. They were covered with golden syrup and eaten very hot. Nothing could be simpler, and this pudding must have been eaten by primitive man, I thought as I grew older. I could see them grinding the wheat ears in a stone quern such as we had in the garden, boiling spring water over an open fire and dropping the wheaten flour into the water in some kind of an iron pot.

Apple Dumplings

Large apples from the orchard were picked in summer, preferably the Keswicks which roasted into a foam of whiteness. Half a pound of flour and three ounces of lard are rubbed together to make into a stiff paste with a little water. Cut into six pieces and roll each one out into a circular shape. Put an apple, pared and cored, on each with a little brown sugar and a clove in the top. Close up and bake for half an hour.

The old name for peel, the outer covering of fruit, vegetables and nuts was rind. We always spoke of the rind of apples and pears, of onions and carrots, as well as of cheese and bacon. It was used in Elizabethan days as when Rosalind says,

'Sweetest nut has sourest rind.'

It was a word we always used, and it occurs throughout the

recipe books. Se we peeled the rind from apples, and now a good honest word has been partly lost.

The rind is the best part of the fruit we were told, and we ate our apples unpeeled. Now I am faced with many little apples, some of them windfalls, some of which have never grown to full size, and it is a nuisance to peel them. I have remembered our old ways and I stew them whole, skin and pips and stalks. They have been well-washed, and as they grow in my own garden I know they have not been sprayed. I use the old recipe of childhood, a recipe I despised.

Green Snow

Take two pounds of small apples, or a dozen of the apples or more, whichever you wish, according to the number of guests. Place them in a deep pan with about four tablespoonfuls of sugar. Add a pint of water and simmer until tender, pushing the top apples down in the pan as they rise. Pour off surplus liquid juice, and spoon the apples into a sieve. Press through, and put the purée in small glass bowls. Pour cream into each bowl and mix well. Then put dabs of whipped cream and ratafia biscuits on the surface. The juice which was removed may be used to make apple jelly, with isinglass. The apple purée has a distinctive flavour owing to the presence of the apple rinds, and the colour is a rich green, from the fresh young apples.

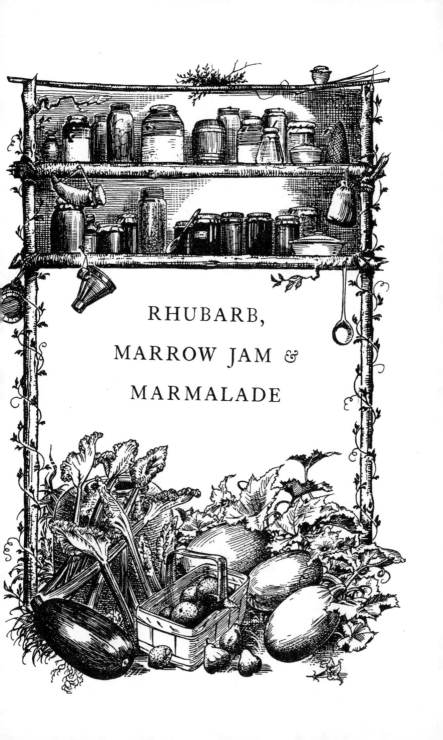

RHUBARB,

MARROW JAM &

MARMALADE

RHUBARB grew in the middle of the garden in a large bed, and it was a source of pride. It was cherry red, and very sweet, and children pulled out a stalk and ate it as modern children eat lollipops. It was the chief food in the games of Robinson Crusoe and we ate it on little paper plates, when we sat at the rustic table on the grass. It was the origin of many recipes, and we never tired of it. It was 'Apple Rhubarb', and we were told that a root of this came to us from a great house and so it had a history.

Rhubarb and Fig Pudding

Make a syrup of half a pound of sugar and half a pint of water and stew in it two pounds of rhubarb and a pound of figs. Make the stewed fruit a nice colour with cochineal. Put alternate layers of bread and fruit in a pie-dish. Let it stand until cold. Turn out and decorate round the top with custard or whipped cream.

Rhubarb Jam

To every pound of fruit peeled and cut up as for tarts, put the same quantity of lump sugar. To about every four pounds of fruit allow a quarter of a pound of bitter almonds, blanched and pounded, the juice of one large lemon, or of two small lemons, and the peel chopped finely. After mixing the fruit with the sugar let it stand all night. Then boil it and when it begins to thicken add the other ingredients. A teaspoonful of ginger is an improvement. Boil for two hours.

This jam, made with either raspberries or figs chopped finely, which are mixed with the rhubarb instead of the almonds, is very good indeed.

We made this jam in vast quantities. It was put in a tall earthenware jar, an ancient brown jar with incised flowers and crosses round the bulging sides, a jar standing about two feet high. It was kept on the stone bench in the pantry, and we had the jam in saucerfuls, with thick cream, eaten with a teaspoon.

Rhubarb Jam, a second recipe

Bruise a piece of whole ginger, and put it in a large earthenware bowl. Slice a lemon and an orange finely. Peel four pounds of rhubarb, and cut it in small slices. Add six pounds of sugar and set all away for twenty-four hours. Strain off the juices and boil them for ten minutes. Pour over the fruit and leave until next day. Then boil all together for half an hour. Bottle and seal.

Finally, the rhubarb was made into a jelly.

Rhubarb Jelly

Stew a pound of ripe rhubarb until tender with enough sugar to sweeten it and a little candied peel and lemon. Put through a sieve and add an ounce of leaf gelatine dissolved in a pint of water. Colour with cochineal and pour into a mould.

Children were devotees of vegetable marrow jam. It was sweet, runny, and golden, and we ate it with a spoon.

Marrow Jam

Cut a hard marrow grown specially for jam, into one inch cubes. As the marrow is hard this is tiring. Put cubes in a bowl with water to cover and leave for twelve hours. Pour half the water away. Put a pound of sugar over the marrow and leave another twelve hours. Then weigh the marrow and use half a pound of sugar to one pound of fruit. Add the juice and rind of a lemon for about every three pounds of marrow and some whole ginger in a muslin bag. Boil gently until the juice is fairly thick and the marrow is tender. Then bottle in warm jars and seal up. The syrup should be clear and golden and the fruit slightly hard and set.

Marmalade (*a small quantity*)

Wash six Seville oranges and one lemon. Peel them and put all the peel into a brass pan with seven pints of water. While it is boiling cut up the pulp and remove the pips. Pour boiling water over the pips. Add the pulp to the orange and lemon peel and boil gently for an hour and a half, until the peel is tender. Cool and cut the peel into fine strips. Return to the saucepan, with the water from soaking the pips, and add seven pounds of sugar. Boil for a quarter of an hour. Stir every now and then. Pour into jars and seal down.

Madeira Marmalade

Use Seville oranges, and slice very thin, taking out the pips. To each pound of fruit add three pints of cold water. Let it stand twenty-four hours. Then boil till the 'chips' are tender. Let it stand until next day. Weigh it and to every pound of boiled fruit add one and a quarter pounds of loaf sugar. If this amount seems too sweet, use only one pound of sugar for each pound of fruit. Boil until the sugar jellies and the 'chips' become transparent. This takes about twenty minutes.

Quinces grew in the garden of a friend at an ancient house, and we were fascinated by the delicate colour and the name Peter Quince, which we met in Shakespeare.

Quince Marmalade

To each pound of fruit use one pound of sugar, a pint of water and a spoonful of brandy. Wipe, peel and cut up the quinces, and leave in cold water to keep the colour. Put the rinds in cold water and boil till tender. Strain off the liquid. When cold put the peeled quince into it, weighing a pound of quince to a pound of sugar to a pint of liquid. Boil all till tender, keeping closely covered. Then beat with a wooden spoon until the right thickness. Pour into warmed pots and cover when cold with brandied paper.

This recipe of the eighteenth century was handed down to me.

EASTER BAKING

& HOME-MADE

BREAD

W H E N Good Friday was near we had great preparations, for often visitors, relations and friends came to see us to tell us the news and to enjoy our food. My mother baked hot cross buns, for they were not sold in the village. Also she made Easter cakes, similar to those which were sold in the shops and made at a little market town in the hills. We made our own Easter cakes as follows, but we often bought a few of these delicate thin trifles which were more professional than our own.

Easter Cakes

Into eight ounces of flour rub four ounces of butter. Add four ounces of sugar, a handful of currants, half a teaspoonful of mixed spice and cinnamon, and a squeeze of lemon. Beat up an egg with a tablespoonful of brandy and mix into the paste. Place on a floured board and, after rolling very thin, cut into rounds about five inches across. Bake in a quick oven and watch carefully lest they get overdone. They should be sweet and crisp.

I associate these little yellow cakes with fresh primroses, picked from our fields, and the first violets from the lane. They should be served with a little bunch of flowers on the top.

Hot Cross Buns

Yeast, which we called barm, was ordered beforehand from the brewery unless the oatcake man had called with some. It was creamed (about an ounce of yeast) with a little sugar and half a pint of milk, and left on the stove to get warm, but never hot. Everybody kept an eye on it lest it got overheated. Then two pounds of flour were mixed with half a pound of sugar and a pound of currants, and some nutmeg was grated on with a little spice. A hole was made in the centre and the warm yeast and milk were poured into this well. A batter was made with this, by drawing in flour from the sides of the well, and the bowl was set before the fire on the great hearth, with a cloth over it to keep draughts away. The mixture began to 'work' with the yeast and as it rose a quarter of a pound of melted butter was poured in. The soft paste was mixed and then covered again and left to continue with rising. When it was ready, and after a finger tip had been used to check the correct texture, the dough was removed to the table and shaped into small round buns. They were spaced on a buttered tin, two inches apart, and put on a high wire rack in the warmth over the fire to rise more, or to 'prove', for half an hour. A cross was cut in each with the back of a knife, and the buns were baked for twenty minutes in a quick oven.

We ate them on Good Friday without butter and without using a knife.

We sang the little old song as we sat down to the meal.
'Hot cross buns. Hot cross buns,
One a penny, two a penny, hot cross buns.
If you don't like them give them to your sons.
If your sons don't like them give them to your daughters,

But if you have none of these little elves,
Then you must eat them all yourselves.'
Any left over were finished off for tea.

At other times we had an unfailing supply of home-made tea cakes, which were for tea and lunches at school and meals for men in the fields. It was a food which was very important, it filled the hungry gaps with a good nourishing meal. They were solid affairs, sweet and good with plenty of fruit and butter, quite unlike any puffy tea-cakes sold in the shops.

Tea Cakes

Two pounds of flour were needed for a batch, and half a pound of good butter. The flour was weighed into a bowl and six or eight ounces of brown sugar was added. A well was made in the middle and an ounce of brewer's yeast, which had been mixed in a pint of warm milk and left on the stove to begin to rise, was added. This made the dough like cream. The bowl was put on the hearth, covered with a white cloth and left to rise. It took about an hour or a little longer and everyone had a peep under the cloth to see how it was getting on. A child would poke a finger in it and be reprimanded. Dough was exciting, a lively white cushion, growing bigger and bigger. The butter was melted, poured in and stirred into the dough. This new dough then was taken out and shaped into little buns which were spaced on a large flat greased tin. They would increase in size so room was left. They were put on the rack over the fire to prove. When they had risen to double their size, about six inches across, they were put in the hot oven and baked.

Sometimes we had candied peel or spice in the buns. They were very tender, and light as a feather, but solid.

We were proud of the tea cakes, which had to have no puffiness or frivolity in them. Years of experience went into their making and I never could make them myself.

On special occasions when somebody was coming to tea we had a thin coating of icing on the buns. Usually they were sliced and toasted and eaten with plenty of butter.

Bread was made at home, about twelve large loaves at a baking. It was kept in the dairy, in an enormous earthenware crock as big as a barrel, and it kept very fresh all week. We often mixed the dough with milk or buttermilk instead of water. The oven was a good baking oven and the bread baked evenly. After a time whoever was in charge of the baking would open the oven door and peep inside to its depths. It was a very large oven and it held many things. She would take out a tin and ease up the loaf and tap on the bottom. She listened, and all was quiet. I listened too, half expecting to hear a voice and to see the loaf door open and a little man appear. Every loaf was tapped before it was taken out and removed from the tin and placed on the dresser. There was a delicious smell which filled the house, and anyone entering gave a big sniff of pleasure.

Home-made Bread

A stone of strong white flour is put in a warmed pancheon, (one of those great yellow and brown pancheons which were so useful in a farmhouse but are seldom seen now). Make a well in the centre and sprinkle in salt, a teaspoonful to each pound of flour, and this must be crushed lump salt, dropped on top of the flour. Three ounces of yeast is mixed with lukewarm water and put on the stove to get slightly warm, when it will begin to 'work'. Pour this barm into the well, sprinkle a teaspoonful of sugar on it and stir with a large spoon. Leave in a warm place for about fifteen minutes. Then mix to a pliable but not sticky dough with the hands, adding milk or water as necessary and kneading for about ten minutes. Knead and mix until the dough leaves the sides of the pancheon. Turn the dough over to make a cushion and leave it, covered with a warm white cloth, on the hearth-stone near the fire. Do not open doors or leave in a draught, but treat the rising dough as if it were human. Bread is the staff of life. Grease several large bread tins. Ours were four-pound tins, bright and clean and heavy, but we had a few two-pounders for loaf cakes. When the dough has risen, and been tested by a finger, it is removed from the pancheon on to the pastry board. Cut off portions and knead them again on the board to form shapes. Put the roundish lumps in the bread tins, to half-fill them, and set to rise again, covered with a cloth, until they are twice the size. Our loaves were placed on a rack which stretched across the whole fireplace and boiler and oven, a useful device. Then bake in a moderate oven till nearly brown. Tap on the bottom of a loaf, tipping it up for a moment to test it. It should sound hollow when ready. Each loaf must be tested in this way. Some people lifted the loaf on the flat of a hand and if it did not burn it was done.

The loaves stood on end to cool in the kitchen for some hours before removing to the cool dairy. There they were stored in the great bread mug. Any little curling crusts were removed and eaten by the children, as 'kissing crust', a lucky feast to have.

Some of the dough from baking was kept for dumplings.

Barm Dumplings

A large saucepan of boiling water was needed. Take some dough from bread-making, and use small portions the size of an apple. Shape into balls and throw into boiling water. Boil till twice the original size. Serve at once, either with golden syrup or sugar and raspberry vinegar, as a winter sweet, or with a stew made of meat.

Dough used as pastry

Take one pound of bread dough and a pound of leaf lard. Knead both together and leave for about an hour to rise before the fire. Then knead again and use as ordinary pastry.

The lard used for pastry was called 'leaf lard', which was finer than ordinary lard, and when separated from scraps of skin could be used easily as it was soft.

The farm delicacy which was well-known among us, was Cobs. They were little round snowballs of bread, the same size as a snowball and just as white and soft, never brown. We had them for tea, piled on a plate and we each took one, cut it and buttered it and ate it.

I have no recipe, my mother always guessed and when I asked how she made them she could not tell me, but she made some to show me.

Cobs (as I think they were made)

Two pounds of fine flour is needed for about twenty cobs. Warm a pint of milk and put in it an ounce of yeast, fresh from the brewer. Add a little salt and put on the stove to warm and to begin to 'work'. Keep from getting hot and watch for the bubbles. Pour this barm into the fine flour in a large bowl and mix well to make a dough. Cover with a clean white cloth and put by the fire to rise for three hours. Turn it out on the baking board and knead it well. Dust with flour and return it to keep warm by the fire, until the dough has risen again and is settled.

Take out and cut off small pieces the size of a tennis ball. Mould them into rounds, let them stand by the fire for a time to prove, covered with a cloth if the room is warm enough. Then brush over with a beaten up egg. Put on a flat dusted tin and bake for about an hour, until the cobs are lightly done, but not brown.

Cobs had a special attraction for me. I thought they were enchanted food, they were so light and airy, so sweet and delicate, they might have been baked in Titania's kitchen in the hazel woods, and my drooping spirits were always raised by the sight of a dish piled with cobs on the white tablecloth when I came home.

SCONES

&

PIKELETS

THERE are several recipes for scones, which we pronounced 'scons'. I was taught to make scones myself when I was young, for it was an easy lesson in cookery.

Plain Scones

Take one pound of flour and a pinch of salt, rub in a scrap of butter the size of a walnut and add a heaped teaspoonful of baking powder. Mix with either sour milk or buttermilk, using enough to make a soft dough. Mix the ingredients well together, roll out, cut into rounds and bake in a flat tin in a quick oven.

Scones, my mother's recipe

Two pounds of flour and a quarter of a pound of butter. Add a dessertspoonful of baking powder and mix with an egg.

Baking powder was made at home of course. It was kept in a large dark green tin with a tight-fitting lid, and it rested on the bottom shelf of the Queen Anne cupboard in the kitchen. It was such an ancient tin I always stared at it as if it belonged to the time of the Romans. I held it in reverence, and carried it carefully with both hands when anyone asked for it. It was a sacred tin with magical properties, changing flour to a quick-rising dough.

Baking Powder

Half a pound of cream of tartar, mixed with a quarter of a pound of bicarbonate of soda. To this add a tablespoonful of ground rice. Dry well in the oven and sift through a fine sieve. Keep in an airtight tin.

Scones, a richer recipe

Two pounds of flour, one cup of sugar and three eggs. Mix with a little warm milk and bake in a hot oven.

A childhood recipe for scones, spaced with red ink and decorated with dots, comes from a manuscript book.

Scones (Sultana)

Half a pound of flour, and one ounce of butter. Mix the flour with one teaspoonful of cream of tartar, and half a teaspoonful of bicarbonate of soda. Rub in the butter and add one ounce of sugar and one ounce of sultanas. Make into a stiff paste with milk. Roll into a round shape and cut into six even parts. Bake in a quick oven.

Caraway Scones

A pound of flour, with a teaspoonful of baking powder, is put into a bowl. Mix with four ounces of butter or lard, and crumble to a fineness. Stir in six ounces of sugar, and two tablespoonfuls of caraway seeds. Make a well in the middle and put in this two tablespoonfuls of marmalade, a teaspoonful of bicarbonate of soda, dissolved, and a tablespoonful of vinegar. Mix to a stiff dough with sour milk. Roll out and cut into rounds. Bake until light brown.

Caraway Seed Bread

Four pounds of flour are mixed with two pounds of sugar creamed with three quarters of a pound of butter. Two ounces of caraway seeds are added to the flour, and three ounces of baking powder. Mix with three eggs and a quart of milk. Bake in bread tins. This quantity makes two large loaves and one small loaf. Leave till cold and slice and well butter.

Pikelets were the delicious thin companions of the oat-cakes, the staple dish instead of bread a hundred years ago. No bread was baked when wheat was so dear at the time of the Corn Laws, and every farmer could grow oats on the poor rocky soil. So great batches of oatcakes were made each week and hung up to dry like brown washing on a line. We adored oatcakes but they were never made at home, for the oatcake man came every fortnight, walking across the hills on mountain paths with his large basket of oatcakes on his arm. He also sold pikelets, which we bought. Oatcakes were toasted and eaten with dripping, pikelets had butter and this was the rule.

Pikelets

Half an ounce of yeast (this was also sold by the oat-cake man, and we bought a little each time he visited us), some flour and a quart of warm milk, a cupful of melted butter and a little salt are needed. Make the milk warm on the top of the stove and stir into it the yeast. This heating of the yeast is important, for the heat has to be low, and a saucepan should not be used. Instead the milk should be put in an enamel or metal bowl to get slightly warm. Then add sufficient flour to make it into a batter. Set it on the hearth-stone to rise before the fire for an hour, and shield from draughts. Then add the butter melted. Stir it well. Pour it into iron rings previously placed on a hot plate or griddle, and bake very lightly on both sides. The colour should be pale gold. It takes five minutes to cook after the top has blistered with bubbles. Leave to cool and dry. Then toast and butter well when hot.

Carsington Pikelets

Half an ounce of cream of tartar and a quarter of an ounce of bicarbonate of soda are mixed with two pounds of flour. Add sugar to taste, and three ounces of melted butter. Beat up six eggs and add two pints of milk, and beat again with the milk. Add this gradually to the flour mixture, dropping it in a hole in the middle and beating slowly. Drop a tablespoonful of this batter on an iron griddle, and allow it to spread. It should be about five inches across and very thin. Turn it when pale brown and bubbly. It should be very light, unlike the Scotch pancake with which it is sometimes confused. It must be cooled on a rack and then toasted very crisp, with plenty of butter added to the bubbled side.

Griddle Scones

A pound of flour, three quarters of an ounce of baking powder, two ounces of lard, and a few currants. Mix with milk and bake on the griddle.

The griddle was a heavy iron plate with a fixed handle, which was used regularly a hundred years ago. It was hung in the brewhouse, and I never saw it in use although I used to hear of the wonderful little flat cakes which were baked on it long ago. It was easy to clean, it was quick and it was used over an open fire. But it was so heavy nobody wished to use it.

CAKES & TEA-TIME
DELICACIES

MARGARINE was unknown, and butter was plentiful, so we bought few cakes or biscuits and made all at home in an oven ever ready.

Although a Lancashire and Cheshire dish, Eccles cakes were a favourite in our county.

Eccles Cakes

Melt one ounce of butter in a saucepan, and add three ounces of currants, two ounces of sugar, half an ounce of candied peel and a little nutmeg. Roll out some good pastry, thin, and cut into rounds. On to each round put a spoonful of the mixture which should be cold. Wet the edges and draw together. Turn over and roll out till the currants start to show through. Make a slit in the top, and bake in the oven for twenty minutes.

We often had a variant of this. The fruit mixture was put in a huge flat pasty and covered with paste. It was baked on a flat tin and when cold cut into narrow fingers.

Tennis Cake

Beat a quarter of a pound of butter with five ounces of sugar to a cream. Add three well-beaten eggs, five ounces of flour, and a teaspoonful of baking powder. Line the tin with greased paper and bake for forty minutes.

Cherry Cake

Beat a quarter of a pound of butter to a cream. Add a quarter of a pound of sugar, and the yolks of two eggs. Add glacé cherries to taste, almonds and peel. Then add the whites of the eggs beaten well, and a quarter of a pound of flour with a teaspoonful of baking powder. Bake in a moderate oven.

Lemon Cream Tartlets

Take two eggs and beat the yolks to a froth. Add a cupful of castor sugar, beating all the time, and the juice of two lemons and the grated peel of one. Line some patty pans with puff paste and just before filling them add a cup of cream to the lemon mixture. Bake until the pastry is cooked and the custard firm. Stand in a cool place. When cold spread over the top a meringue made of the whites of the eggs whipped with two tablespoonfuls of castor sugar. Put the tartlets in a slow oven to set the meringue.

The cool place in our house for setting such delicacies as lemon cream tartlets, or jellies or custard, was on the stone wall outside the back door. There was a large flat stone, where they were left to cool in the wild north winds which always seemed to blow there. Perhaps the squirrels eyed the dishes from the nut trees or the birds fluttered near but the human beings in the house kept a watch from the window and the tasty dishes were undisturbed by marauders.

Our Custard

The custard with this laconic title is made as follows. A quart of milk, a little lemon peel, a stick of cinnamon, a little sugar and three eggs. Heat the milk with the flavourings and sugar. Stir in the beaten eggs but do not boil afterwards. Stir again until the custard is cold.

I was the stirrer always. I took the bowl to the back door and put it on the stone wall where it was flat. Then I stirred with a wooden spoon while my eye roamed over the marvellous view of the hills and fields and woods, with the tree tops below me in the hollow of the hill.

Mechanically my arm stirred the bowl of custard and my mind was free to wander with hawks and rabbits, with squirrels and corncrake.

Swiss Roll

This well-known roll was a great excitement to us when we first saw it made. It was so different in shape from all the cakes and tartlets we had seen. Four eggs and six ounces of castor sugar are put in a bowl over boiling water and whisked until warm and thick. Then the bowl is removed from the heat and the mixture whisked until cool. Mix in four ounces of flour with a quarter of a teaspoonful of baking powder, very lightly, adding vanilla flavouring and lemon rind cut fine. Spread thinly on a baking sheet which has been buttered and dusted with sugar and flour. Bake in a quick oven, turn out and spread with jam very quickly, and roll up.

Sponge Cake

Take five eggs, new laid. Take the weight of two and a half eggs in flour. Put half a pound of sifted sugar in a bowl and break the five eggs into it. Beat half an hour. Then stir the flour lightly in, but do not beat any more. Pour into a buttered tin lined with paper and bake gently for an hour. It will rise high.

This cake was a stand-by; there always seemed to be a fresh one newly baked, ready for children and visitors who called to see us.

We had fruit bread spread with butter for tea, and it was a popular sweet for farm men. There was a rich version and a plainer one for everyday.

Fruit Bread

Take two pounds of flour, and rub in half a pound of butter. Add half a pound of Demerara sugar, one and a half pounds of currants, a few raisins, some candied peel, a pint of milk altogether, a teaspoonful of bicarbonate of soda, dissolved in a little of the milk, and a teaspoonful of baking powder. Bake in a moderate oven, in a loaf tin, for three hours.

Fruit Bread, a second recipe

Two pounds of flour, and half a pound of lard. Add one pound of currants, two ounces of almonds, blanched and chopped, one pound of sugar, and half a pound of raisins. Add one ounce of baking powder and mix with milk. Bake in a fairly hot oven. Serve with butter.

Sugar Biscuits

Work into a stiff paste one pound of butter, one pound of sugar, one pound of flour and two eggs. Roll out, cut into rounds and bake in a quick oven.

This was a biscuit kept in a large tin in the Dark Passage ready for a glass of home-made wine and a visit from vicar, insurance man, traveller's agent for corn and meal, poor old ladies and ancient uncles.

Birthday Cake

Half a pound of butter and half a pound of sugar creamed together. Add three eggs and beat well. Stir in half a pound of flour, half a pound of currants or sultanas, and two ounces of candied peel. Pour into a greased tin and bake for two hours in a very moderate oven.

Cover the top with icing as desired.

Mrs. Lowe's Little Cakes

Two cups of flour and one cup of sugar are mixed with three quarters of a cup of creamy milk fresh from the cow. Work a little yeast, warmed in milk, into the flour, add fruit to taste and bake in a flat tin in heaps like rock buns.

Chocolate Icing

Grate four ounces of chocolate, mix with four ounces of icing sugar, a few drops of vanilla and a tablespoonful of water. Stir over the fire until melted. Do not let it boil. Pour over the cake.

Shortbread

One pound of flour, half a pound of butter and a quarter of a pound of sugar. Cream the butter, gradually add the flour and sugar. Work up to a paste. Roll to a thick round, and mark the edge with a finger print. Make slight cuts across the centre to divide it into six pieces. Sprinkle sugar over it and bake.

Jane's Buns

Put eight ounces of flour and a teaspoonful of baking powder, some salt and nutmeg into a bowl. Rub three ounces of butter into it till it is like bread-crumbs. Add four ounces of sugar, a little mixed fruit and orange peel. Beat in an egg, stirring all the time. Place portions in bun tins, and cook in a coolish oven for twenty minutes.

Castleton Vicarage Cake

A pound of white flour is put in a bowl and three quarters of a pound of Demerara sugar, a pound of mixed currants and sultanas, and a quarter of a pound of candied peel are added. Mix together and make a well in the middle. Cut three quarters of a pound of butter into small pieces, sprinkle on a teaspoonful of bicarbonate of soda, and pour a little boiling milk over this. Pour into the well and mix. Bake in a moderate oven about two hours. This cake will keep for weeks and it improves with keeping.

Castleton is a village in the hills where we used to drive to visit our friends and spend wonderful days at a farm.

Lunch Cake

A pound and a half of flour is mixed with half a pound of dripping, or butter, and half an ounce of home-made baking powder. Half a pound of brown sugar is added and half a pound of currants and a little salt. Candied peel or grated lemon rind can be added if liked. Mix with about half a pint of milk to which a little flavouring, vanilla or a pinch of cinnamon, has been added. Bake in a fairly hot oven.

Currant Cakes

These big cakes were made when large numbers of people were coming to tea. Seven pounds of flour are mixed with three pounds of butter. Then two pounds of sultanas, and three pounds of currants are added, with two pounds of sugar, and four ounces of baking powder. Beat up with a quart of milk. Make into three or four cakes in cake tins well buttered.

Every year in late autumn, when the days were shortening and we were prepared to be snowbound, we had a final festival, to cheer us for the coming darkness of night with candles and lanterns. It was Wakes Week, with the merry-go-rounds and swing boats, the hawkers with their stalls, when the ribbons and gingerbread were sold and fireworks were thrown in the air. Then we had Wakes cakes. This is the recipe.

Wakes Cakes

Half a pound of butter is worked into threequarters of a pound of flour. Six ounces of white sugar are added, with half a teaspoonful of baking powder and some currants, a handful, and some caraway seeds and lemon peel. These are beaten with a well-beaten egg, and mixed to a paste not too thin. Roll out and cut into rounds about four inches across. Sprinkle the surfaces with sugar and bake quickly. They should be crisp and sweet like biscuits.

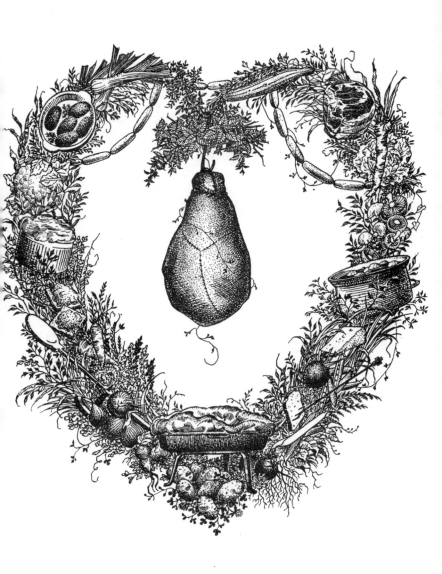

SAVOURY DISHES

OCTOBER was the month for roasting potatoes in their jackets. There was a square embroidered piece of linen with the words 'Roast Potatoes' in many colours of cross-stitch embroidered across a corner. The roast potatoes were taken from the oven and folded in this and placed on a dish. We ate them for supper, with teaspoons, not a knife and fork, and with them we had fresh farm butter, and a jug of cream, and salt. We poured the cream into a hole in the half potato, and dropped butter and salt in too. We finished by eating the skin, for we had grown the potatoes and kept them in store ready for winter's use and we must not waste anything. Children at school chanted a rhyme:

'Dearly beloved brethren, isn't it a sin
To eat roast potatoes and throw away the skin?
The skin feeds pigs and the pigs feed you.
Dearly beloved brethren—don't you think it's true?'

Some of the tasty dishes for supper included cheese.

A Preparation of Cheese

Peel, cut up and boil two large onions. When quite soft, drain and chop fine. (We did this with a chopper of ancient

shape, a semicircle of fine sharp steel mounted on a handle.)
Grate a quarter of a pound of cheese, and add to the onion.
Also add a cupful of cream and two ounces of butter.
Simmer in a pan and serve on buttered toast.

The pan for this delicacy was made of brass, a heavy
saucepan, polished bright with sandstone, for no patent
cleaners were used. The toast was of course made in front
of the fire, with a long-handled large toasting fork, the
handle about two feet long as the fire was so hot.

Cheese pudding, or savoury, was another supper dish.

Cheese Pudding

A piece of butter is melted into two tablespoonfuls of
flour and half a pound of cheese, grated, is added, with
salt, pepper and mustard. Beat up two or three eggs, and
mix with the other ingredients. Then add a cupful of
cream. Mix gently, and put in a buttered dish. Bake for
twenty-five minutes.

Scotch Woodcock

Mix in a pan two ounces of grated parmesan cheese,
one and a half teaspoonfuls of anchovy paste, half a teacupful of cream, and a pinch of cayenne pepper. Let it melt
and just come to the boil. Then spread it on three slices
of hot toast and serve.

Cheese Soufflé

Melt an ounce of butter in a little milk (about a quarter
of a pint), and add half an ounce of flour to thicken. Cool
and beat in the yolk of an egg and two or three ounces of
finely grated cheese. Then beat the whites of two eggs and
fold in carefully, not beating. Pour the mixture into a buttered fireproof dish, and bake in a hot oven for a quarter of

an hour, or until set. Sprinkle with cheese and brown before the fire, or use the red hot salamander to brown the cheese.

The salamander was used for all browning purposes, for we had no grill, and it was easy to heat the iron in the fire.

Toad in the Hole

This well-known dish, with its intriguing title, was served now and then for supper. A batter was made from six ounces of plain flour and two eggs, which were dropped into the centre and beaten. A pint of milk was added gradually and the batter was left to rest for half an hour at least. Then it was turned into a hot greased earthenware dish about an inch deep in which a few sausages were placed. It was put in the oven, baked for about half an hour and served in the dish.

Exeter Stew

Fry one pound of beef steak, cut into pieces, and one sliced onion with one ounce of dripping until brown. Make a sauce with one ounce of flour, browned in the fat in the pan, salt and pepper and one pint of water or stock, and add to the meat with one or two sliced carrots. Bring to the boil and then simmer for one and a half hours, or more, adding dumplings after the first threequarters of an hour.

Dumplings

One teacup of flour, two tablespoonfuls of suet, a dessertspoonful of parsley chopped, salt and pepper, half a teaspoonful of baking powder. Make these into a paste with a little water. Shape into six dumplings and drop gently into the boiling water with the meat.

Beef Croquettes

A cupful of minced cold beef is mixed with a quarter of a cupful of cold mashed potato, and seasoned with pepper, salt and onion juice and minced parsley. Add enough gravy to moisten and a raw egg to bind it. Work together well, and mould into balls or cones. Cover with egg and bread-crumbs and fry.

Boiled beef was eaten with suet pudding made with herbs. Roast sirloin had Yorkshire pudding, rising to a height, crisp and soft and golden.

Herb Pudding

The herb pudding for the boiled beef had two handfuls of flour and a handful of chopped beef suet and a teaspoon-ful of bicarbonate of soda. Into this a collection of chopped herbs was tumbled—parsley, thyme and dandelion, young nettles and onions, marjoram and a sprig of fennel. It was mixed with a beaten egg and the pudding put in a greased basin, and boiled or steamed for two hours. It was served with the boiled beef and cut in slices.

Roast beef was served with horseradish sauce and with a batter pudding, only sometimes called Yorkshire, in deference to an argumentative aunt.

The sirloin was always the best cut, chosen with care and enquiries about the origin of the poor animal and the farm from which it had come. This always distressed me, for I knew the fields and cattle so well I did not like to remember the gentle animals were eaten. So I ate with reluctance, concealing my woes.

Horseradish Sauce

This was made by my father, for nobody else could bear the strong tear-compelling horseradish. A stick of it was dug up in the garden and washed and cleaned. Then the root was scraped on an ancient grater which hung on the wall. The ivory shreds were very pungent and we kept away. They were put in a bowl and mixed with white sugar, vinegar and a cup of thick cream.

Yorkshire Pudding

Put four ounces of sieved flour in a bowl, and a pinch of salt. Make a well in the centre and into this drop two eggs. Mix in the flour, allowing it to drop from the well sides, until the whole is absorbed. Then add slowly half a pint of milk, beating gently with a wooden spoon. Add a tablespoonful of water. Keep beating when the mixture is smooth and beat longer till bubbles form. Cover and leave for an hour. In a fairly deep meat tin place some dripping and make it hot in the oven. Pour in the batter and return quickly to the oven to cook. For the last few minutes, when it has risen, it should be placed on a trivet in front of a hot fire to set.

This was served with the beef, turned out on a dish to itself and then cut for each person.

The same pudding was served with roast pork but in this case some herbs were added to the batter before cooking. We added some chopped onion and chopped sage, thyme and parsley, to make a savoury dish.

Sometimes the Yorkshire pudding was served alone with butter and sugar as a sweet, but I always felt defrauded when in other houses this happened. We stuck to the old regime of Roast Beef and Yorkshire.

Mushrooms were the magical fruits of the pastures and each morning in the season the servant boy would find a few fresh pinky-gilled mushrooms when he went to the fields to call up the cows. We went again later in the day,

for new mushrooms had already sprung up in that miracu-
lous way which always astonishes the country-bred people
who are used to slow growth and invisible changes.

Mushrooms in Cream

When the mushrooms were brought to the kitchen they
were peeled at once and the tips cut from their stalks, and
then they were put convex side down into a saucer or two
of cream. Salt and pepper was sprinkled over them and the
saucers were placed at once in the hot oven. They were
cooked and were ready for the early breakfast. They were
poured over hot buttered toast and they made a 'dish fit
for a king'. We never ate them with bacon, and we never
fried them, for then the delicate flavour would be lost.
We had mushrooms for tea, from an afternoon's picking,
but they were always cooked in china saucers, to retain the
flavour. At tea-time we ate them with bread and butter
straight from the saucers in which they were cooked.

To cure a Ham

A pound and a half of common salt was needed, and a
pound of bay salt, two ounces of saltpetre, a quarter of a
pound of black pepper, a pound and a half of juniper berries from our own little juniper bush, a pound of Demerara
sugar and two pounds of black treacle, also a quart of ale
from the brewery, and specially old ale was used. The ingredients were bruised together in a large brown vessel,
and boiling water was poured over them. The ham lay in
this pickle about a month, turned every day and basted and
examined. Then it was put in a calico bag and hung in the
kitchen from a hook in the ceiling for six months or more.
The hook was behind a certain door where the ham would
not hit anyone's head. It received the full impact of wood

smoke and the scents of herbs, and of ordinary life, to cure it.

It was simmered in an enormous iron pan with a round fixed handle and a lid, and herbs were put in the water. Then when cooked it was skinned hot and covered with breadcrumbs. Every farm had its own recipe for curing a ham, using different kinds of herbs and sweetenings, some using black treacle only, others Demerara sugar.

BEVERAGES

EACH spring there was a small expedition to pick cowslips for wine. The cowslip field was a favourite meadow,
kept for mowing, but although it was not to be entered in
high summer we could go there in early spring to pick the
cowslips which made the grass golden. It was a delightful
experience, a magical time of life, to wander in that delectable place, with its underground spring and its water-
trough, its hedges of wild honeysuckle with red campion
underneath, and its cowslips, freckled, spotted with scarlet,
large and small. I looked intently at everything and I was
charmed by these flowers, among which I often found an
oxlip—then I held it in my hands, shut my eyes and made
a wish.

One morning in April my mother would announce that
we would pick cowslips for cowslip wine. We would set
off after breakfast, the servant girl, my brother, my mother
and I, with a clothes-basket, and several smaller baskets.
It was exciting to run down the first big field, deep down
to the gate that led to the cowslip field. By the gate we left
the clothes-basket, and we each took another basket and
began to gather the flowers. The air was scented, sweet,

aromatic, and the birds sang joyously. We stooped low and picked the flowers, leaving the small ones and gathering those with long stalks and a multitude of bells.

Sometimes we held up a gigantic flower, the queen of all, to show my mother, who smiled at our excitement. She wore a lilac sunbonnet on her dark hair and she looked young and happy as she felt the freedom of the fields and she listened to the birds. On April 14th, usually, the cuckoo came and he always flew to a naked ash tree in the hedge nearby and called to us. So we answered, and the echo called too.

With the cowslips grew blue violets and pearly wood anemones, with little black chimney-sweepers which the fairies used to sweep their chimneys. I secretly kept a sharp look-out for an elf among the cowslips, for it seemed a reasonable place for one to be swinging on the golden bells. Did little Will Shakespeare pick cowslips for wine when he spied the cinque spots in the bell?

We emptied our baskets into the clothes-basket, one after another, but we got tired, our heads were dazed with stooping to the ground. We struggled on, and at last we children were sent off to swing. We climbed up the fields and rested on the swing, dawdling idly, and recovering from the work. After a time, my mother and the maid came up the hill with the basket nearly full between them. Their work continued after a hasty meal, and all afternoon they picked the flowers. When the men went milking they stopped and brought the second load of flowers to the house. The scent from the big loads of cowslips was exquisite, it flowed round us as we breathed it in the dairy.

At night we sat in the kitchen pulling the peeps from the flowers. The stalks and calyces like pale green lace were thrown on a sheet spread on the floor. The 'peeping'

continued all evening, until bedtime, when it was finished.
Then the real making of the wine began.

Cowslip Wine

Measure the peeps of the flowers. To each peck (ours
were measured in the old wooden peck-measuring vessel),
allow three gallons of spring water. To each gallon add
three pounds of sugar. Boil the water and sugar one hour
and skim. Add a few whites of egg whilst boiling. Strain,
cool, and when just warm add a little brewer's yeast. Let it
stand. (Ours stood on the dairy floor in the great tin
pancheon till morning.) Pour in the peeps and the peel of
two lemons to every gallon of liquid. Stir now and then for
nine days. Then pour it into a wooden barrel. Let it be a
fortnight before fastening the bung hole with a cork,
wired on. In two months you may bottle. At the last put
in a pint of best brandy to each three gallons of liquid.

The cowslip wine was bottled towards the winter, and
kept in a cool place. The wine was yellow, resembling
sherry, and the taste was delicious, said those who drank it
from the long pointed glasses which were my grandmother's. We used it sparingly, as it could be intoxicating
and it was expensive to make.

Rhubarb Wine

Cut the rhubarb into pieces without removing the red
skin. Put it in a pitcher and cover with cold water. Let it
stand ten days. Strain and add one pound of moist sugar
to each quart of juice. Let it stand another ten days. Then
bottle it, giving it time to work over the top before cork-
ing. Fill it up as it works out. Cork it in about three days.
Then it is ready for use.

I never tasted this rhubarb wine, which was not so

popular with our family. The great drink for summer was Herb Beer, made from the herbs of the hedgerows—the goosegrass, the nettles, the fruits and plants gathered by an old man who knew all about this beverage. It was brewed in a large tin pancheon, which stood on the dairy floor with pieces of brewer's yeast on toast floating on the surface, making a white bubbling foam. We dipped our little china mugs into it and an enamel mug for the servant boy and we all drank, licking our lips, blinking our eyes against the potency of ginger and fizziness.

Nettles were used on many occasions, for broth, for a vegetable as well as for herb beer. The nettles were gathered by someone wearing leather gloves, when the shoots were about three inches high, young and fresh and pale green. The spiked and barbed leaves, which stung me often as I walked through woods and wild patches of pasture and ploughfield, were tamed by hot water. A basketful would be brought to the house, and the nettles were washed and picked over for cleanliness. Of course only nettles growing in a private and special piece of ground, such as the orchard or a croft not used by animals, were picked. They were washed in salted water, and chopped roughly. Then they were boiled in beef stock, with pearl barley added, for nettle broth. They were boiled in clean cold water for a vegetable like spinach, when they were chopped and rubbed through a sieve, and butter was put on the top.

For herb beer they were chopped and mixed with the brew of cleavers or goosegrass, ginger root, sugar, and herbs from the herb garden, mint, thyme and horehound, fennel, dandelion roots grated, a little sour sorrel, and wood sorrel leaves, salad burnet, cloves and cinnamon.

In all cases the nettles had to be very young and tender,

and only the nettle tips used, not the lower coarser leaves.
The picker of nettles, if stung, should apply dock leaves
to the skin.

Chaddesden Barley Water

A tablespoonful of pearl barley is scalded, and the water
thrown away. The barley is put in a large basin, and the
peel of four lemons and eight lumps of sugar are added.
Two quarts of boiling water are poured over this. Cover
and leave to get cold. When cold pour slowly into a jug
but do not strain off the sediment. Then add the juice of
an extra lemon and drink for colds.

This barley was used in the hayfields for hot men to
slake their thirsts. We made a great deal and it was sent
out in gallon jugs or bottles. A drink of barley water was
also given to horses, for a treat.

Recipes for harvest drinks were important. In thin
spidery gently sloping script I find these almost indeciph-
erable writings by my mother. The ink is so faded, the
writing so tired, I am sure she was weary when she wrote
them by candlelight.

Slackers

Slackers is the best drink for hard work, to slake the
thirst. It is very strengthening. Into a pan put a quarter of
a pound of oatmeal, fine as flour, about six ounces of loaf
sugar, and half a lemon cut into slices. Mix all together
with a little warm water. Then add a gallon of boiling
water, stir thoroughly and use when cool.

Drink for bottling

Dissolve two pounds of loaf sugar in a quart of boiling
water. Add two ounces of citric acid and two sliced lemons.

Stir together and bottle when cold. Take a tablespoonful to a tumbler of water.

Lemonade

One pound of loaf sugar, one ounce of cream of tartar and two lemons cut in slices, in a very large jug. Pour over all three quarts of boiling water.

Ginger Beer

Pour a gallon of boiling water over one pound of loaf sugar. Add one ounce of bruised ginger and two lemons sliced and a few cloves. When lukewarm add one tablespoonful of yeast. Let it stand for twelve hours. Then bottle it. This is a good gingerbeer for the hayfield.

A good drink for Harvest

Boil half an ounce of hops, half an ounce of bruised ginger and a sprig of mint in a gallon and a half of water, for twenty minutes. Add one pound of best Demerara sugar and boil ten minutes more. Then strain, and bottle while hot. It will be ready for drinking when cold.

In the winter we often had possets. We had possets at Christmas, and New Year, possets when we were ill and possets when we were starved (which is to say that we were frozen stiff from the weather, and not that we were hungry). A starved child was a very cold child and I came home from my long walk from school starved in the winter nights. Then I had a posset of hot milk and bread cut into little squares, with a dash of rum and some brown sugar to bring the colour to my cheeks.

Men had possets, stronger, with rum or brandy, to revive them.

'We will have a posset at the end of a sea-coal fire,' says

Shakespeare and we had possets by our own coal fire, from the coal dug in our own county.

Milk was curdled with ale to make a Christmas posset. Spices were added, cloves and cinnamon, and a grate of nutmeg and brown sugar. The posset was mulled on the hot stove, in a pewter tankard, and poured into smaller mugs of pewter when it was ready. The ale curdled the milk and made a froth like 'lamb's wool', the old froth of roast apples once used in possets.

CREAM
CHEESE

Cheeses were made in all the farms until the railway was built in the valley and it was easier and more profitable to sell the liquid milk direct to the towns. The old cheese presses still stood in the barn, with their great stones and vast wooden screws, but only a few farms then made cheese. At Christmas we made a milk cheese and put layers of finely chopped sage through it. This green cheese was a Christmas dainty, for we enjoyed the stripes of green that appeared.

All through the year we made cream cheese, using the following method.

Cream Cheese

Cream that had gone sour was saved, and hung in a muslin bag in a cold window to drain, for a day or two. The resultant curd was flavoured with salt and pepper, and shaped into a square cake. It was placed under a two pound weight for a night, wrapped in hazel leaves in extra muslin. Then it was wrapped in a thick piece of white cloth and buried in the garden about a foot deep. It was left there for three or four days, dug up, and the wrappings removed. It made a delicious cheese.

Cream cheese was always served on three or four large hazel leaves, picked fresh from the tree which overhung the water trough. I was the gatherer of these leaves, and I chose carefully the prettiest green leaves I could reach. They were used as a doily to add to the beauty of the cheese.

The rich milk given by a cow after calving is called 'beestings'. It was much prized and we took little cans of 'beestings' to friends when we drove out to different houses. This rich milk was yellow with cream. It was not drunk, though the calf had some of it. It was used to make a delectable pastry-cake.

Beestings Cakes

A pint of beestings was put in a pie-dish and a pinch of salt and a little sugar added. It was placed in a cool oven to solidify. Then currants were mixed with the curd. This creamy curd was poured into cases of pastry, as separate tarts, and baked; or a large tin was lined with good pastry, the sides being about three inches deep. Into this case the curd was poured and the pastry baked. It was kept in the dairy to become ice-cold and then it was cut in wedges.

Cheese Cakes

These cakes were not unlike the beestings cakes above, but they were made with ordinary rich creamy milk. To a pint of milk, warm from the cow, or slightly heated on the fire, a teaspoonful of rennet was added. The curds left were strained off in muslin. To this was added a quarter of a pound of butter, two eggs beaten up with brandy and a little sugar, and the juice and grated rind of a lemon. Some patty pans were lined with good pastry, and the mixture was poured in, with a few currants added, and baked. In some places these cakes were called 'Maids of Honour', but with us they were simply 'Cheese cakes', although they had nothing to do with cheese, except that curds are akin to cheese. Nutmeg was grated on the surface.

Cheese cakes were eaten for dinner or tea, they were present at every well-filled table, a delicacy which was digestible and popular, creamy and faintly sweet.

Egg Cheese Cakes

Boil four eggs hard and grate them. Add half a pound of sugar, half a pound of butter and half a pound of currants. Put the mixture, flavoured with lemon, in tartlet cases of good pastry and bake.

Rice Cheese Cakes

Melt two ounces of butter and mix it with two ounces of rice flour. Add two ounces of fine sugar, and vanilla to taste. If more flour is needed add a pinch of baking powder. Put into pastry cases and bake.

Sugar Cheese Cakes

Melt a quarter of a pound of butter. Mix it with a quarter of a pound of fine sugar and a quarter of currants. Add a tablespoonful of rum and some lemon peel. Bake in pastry cases till brown.

Cheese cakes were very popular in our household, and there was a baking each week.

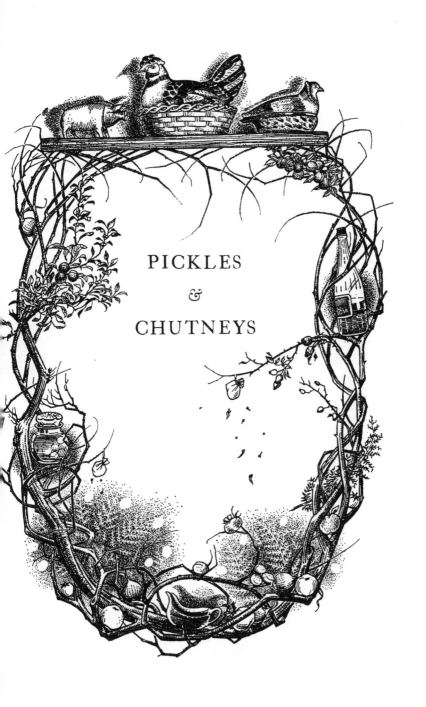

PICKLES

&

CHUTNEYS

PICKLES and chutneys were in demand, for much cold roast beef was eaten, and all pickles were made at home. With cold roast sirloin, or cold roast pork, we had many delicious varieties, using walnuts and damsons, mixed pickles, onions, apples . . .

Damson pickle was a favourite, and damsons were common as blackberries. They grew on old trees which were blue with fruit, in waste places. The trees had been planted a hundred years before round the garden of the pig-cote, along the wall of the orchard, and along the edge of the ploughfield. We had damson jam and damson cheese, and damson pickles and even then the fruit dropped to the ground.

Walnut pickle was another favourite and the walnuts grew in an avenue of trees at a neighbouring farm, trees that had been planted by my grandfather's brother, Great-Uncle Timothy. A basketful of green walnuts was sent to us, and the great task of pricking the nuts with darning needles was begun. It made the hands stained and nobody liked the work.

We had some enormous brown jars, which reminded me of the jars where the Forty Thieves were hidden. They

were kept in a barn but when washed and filled with
pickles they stood on the bench in the pantry. They were
rather beautiful, with two ears and a curling rim and a
tapering body, and some had crosses and roses.

Nobody bought pickles and sauces, and we were busy
in the autumn making pickles either from our own recipes
or from those recommended by friends.

Miss Milward's Pickled Damsons

Take seven pounds of dry sound damsons. Remove the
stalks but not the stones of the fruit. Place the fruit in layers
in a large jar. Sprinkle each layer with sugar. Four pounds of
preserving sugar is needed. Add a quarter ounce of stick
cinnamon and three quarters of an ounce of whole cloves.
Cover with vinegar, and place the jar in a saucepan of
boiling water on the stove. Cook gently until the juice
flows freely. Then put the jar aside until the contents are
quite cold. Drain the syrup into a saucepan and bring to
boiling point. Pour it over the fruit. Repeat this draining
and boiling for seven or eight days, when the skins should
be hard and the damsons have a clear appearance. After
the last boiling, let the damsons remain in the large jar
for seven days. Then transfer to some small jars. Boil the
syrup left and pour it over the fruit in the small jars. Cover
with bladder or paper brushed with white of egg on both
sides. If stored in a dry place the damsons may be kept for
years.

Cherries may be pickled in the same way, but we never
pickled ours for the blackbirds got there first.

Pickled Walnuts

Pick over the basket of walnuts and reject any fruit that
is too hard. A darning needle must be able to pierce the

skin which covers the nut. It takes many hours to pierce a quantity of walnuts and the brown stain is difficult to remove. Place the pricked walnuts in a deep jar, and cover with cold brine made of salt boiled with water, (about six ounces of salt to a quart). Change the brine every four days, and leave for nine days. Then take the nuts and spread them on a large dish. Leave on a bench in the sun to dry and to go black. Then put them in smaller jars. Pour spiced vinegar over them, leave three days then drain them and reboil the vinegar and pour over again. Cover and keep in a dry place.

The spiced vinegar is made from three onions, a pinch of cloves, some peppercorns, allspice, ginger and mace, and a few bay leaves, to half a gallon of vinegar. Boil and strain and then use.

Marrow Chutney, *a country cottage recipe*

One pound of sugar is used to four pounds of marrow when peeled and cut into pieces. Put the pieces on a large dish and sprinkle with a little salt. Let it stand twenty-four hours. Then drain off all liquid and put the marrow in a large preserving pan. Add three pints of vinegar. Mix together half an ounce each of ginger, dry mustard and turmeric powder with a little cold vinegar and add to the marrow in the pan. In a muslin bag put spices, consisting of six chillies and half a dozen cloves. Lastly add two dozen shallots cut up fine. Boil all for one hour slowly. When cool turn into jars and eat with cold meats. There is a disagreeable smell while this is cooking.

Apple Chutney

Take six large sour apples, to be chopped finely with three onions. Add six ounces of sultanas or raisins, chopped roughly. Take the following ingredients: ground ginger, a teaspoonful, cayenne pepper, a saltspoonful, and a dessertspoonful of salt, a tablespoonful of tomato sauce, or the pulp of three tomatoes, a dessertspoonful of anchovy essence, and one of Indian soy, and a tablespoonful of salad oil, all these ingredients and also the others to be put into a mortar and pounded together. By degrees add a tablespoonful of vinegar. When all is well blended put into a wide-mouthed bottle and cork tightly.

Tomatoes were a strange and exotic fruit which we treated with circumspection, for it grew in greenhouses and although it resembled a ripe apple the taste was quite different. So after one bite at the rosy fruit I refused all tomatoes in youth. Sometimes a basket of green tomatoes was sent to us by a friend who had a greenhouse, and we made pickle, which was delectable.

Green tomato pickle

Cut two and a half pounds of green tomatoes in slices and sprinkle salt over this. Let it stand twenty-four hours. Drain and put in a saucepan with vinegar to cover. Add a quarter of a pound of sliced onions, a quarter of a pound of moist sugar and a quarter of a pound of pickling spices, with a few cloves, in a muslin bag. Boil for fifteen minutes, then cool and bottle. If this recipe seems too hot use half the amount of pickling spice. The muslin bag must be removed from the pickle before bottling.

A sauce for salads

Make a gill of good butter sauce (white sauce). Season with salt and pepper, and add the yolk of an egg, a teaspoonful of cream, a few drops of tarragon and chilli vinegar, and lemon juice to taste. This makes an easy sauce

for the salads which also go with cold meat and which can
be made much more colourful and infinitely more inter-
esting by the addition of other vegetables and fruits. We
always used a fresh lettuce, newly picked from the garden,
washed in spring water and dried by shaking in a wire
basket. This lettuce was pulled apart and the leaves placed
in a large old glass dish like a fan. On them lay tomatoes
from the greenhouse of our friend through the woods,
and cucumber slices, small onions grated, spring onions
from the garden, a carrot grated, mixed with an apple
peeled and cut into small bits, a pear also cut up small,
some endive, a sprig of tarragon, and a sprig of fresh mint.

SWEETMEATS

WE seldom bought any sweets, or 'goodies' as we called them, so we had home-made toffee instead. It was very good but very sticky. When we were left alone in the kitchen in care of the maid we asked her to let us make goodies, and she usually agreed. We made inroads in the butter and burned the utensils, but we were happy as we measured and weighed the ingredients and proud of our results.

Everton Toffee

Boil a cup of water with a pound of Demerara sugar very gently until the sugar is dissolved. Then add half a pound of butter. Beat all together for half an hour. Turn out on a buttered tin.

Treacle Toffee

Boil half a pound of treacle with half a pound of Demerara sugar and two ounces of butter. Boil for half an hour. Then test in a cup of cold water, and if it hardens it is done. Pour out on a well-buttered flat dish and cut in squares.

Peppermint Toffee

Boil a pound of treacle very gently with two ounces of best butter and stir to prevent sticking. Boil until it hardens when tested in water. Add a small teaspoonful of essence of peppermint. Pour into well-buttered dishes and cut.

Nut Toffee

Boil half a pound of Demerara sugar with three ounces of butter, the juice of a lemon and a tablespoonful of water. Boil for twenty minutes stirring all the time. Test in cold water. If done drop in a pint of chopped nuts. Stir them in thoroughly and pour into a buttered dish.

Farmhouse Toffee

A pound of raw sugar is put into a pan containing half a pound of melted butter. Add two small tablespoonfuls of treacle, and half a teaspoonful of ginger. Stir all the time while cooking and add the juice of a lemon drop by drop. Boil for ten minutes. Then test in cold water. Just before it is done add two ounces of blanched and split almonds. Pour into a well-buttered dish.

These toffees, made on cold winter days when we could not go out to the fields to play, were a source of pleasure in many ways. The toffees were cooked in a brass saucepan, which did not burn easily, and we cooked over a clear bright fire. We stirred the mixtures with a long-handled wooden spoon, kept in the oak spoon-box on the dresser and we weighed everything with care, using a great ancient set of scales. All the things were spread out on the white scrubbed top of the big table, and we gave cries of delight as we saw the little hot drop of toffee fall into the ice-cold water in an enamel mug and curl to the bottom in a hard wisp. It was an enchantment to see this miracle of hard toffee formed from our mixture.

We had to be tidy and neat, for everything must be cleared away before any man came to the kitchen, for hot water or food for animals. Our recreation was not allowed to interfere with real work.

The making of popcorn was a special joy for we read about this delicacy in American books.

Popcorn

The corn must be popped over a clear fire in a little iron basket with a long handle. The corn is put in the basket and shaken continuously and in time each grain pops suddenly and becomes a little irregular white ball. These fluffy balls can be eaten with salt, or rolled in a sweet syrup, coloured and flavoured, made of white sugar boiled for ten minutes with a little water.

There was a vogue among us for America, perhaps we had just discovered that country across the sea in reading Beulah and Huckleberry Finn and all the tales of Red Indians which filled our minds with fears as we walked through the woods. I find another American recipe in my handwriting of this early stage of life.

American Caramel

Put a teacupful of brown sugar into an old frying pan, says my recipe, (but we always used our brass pans). Stir over the fire for ten minutes adding a piece of butter the size of half an egg. Also add half a cup of milk. Spread very quickly on sandwich cake after adding a few drops of vanilla. Use it instead of jam in the cake.

Coconut Cream

Take a coconut and break it open. Keep the milk ready. Grate the fresh coconut ready for the toffee. Put a pound of loaf sugar with half a cup of coconut-milk in a saucepan and add an ounce of butter. Boil and add the grated coconut, slowly. Boil for ten minutes, stirring all the time. Pour into a basin and beat with fork till nearly cold. Then turn into a dish. Colour half of the mixture pink. Press one half over the other and cut into strips.

This coconut cream was made into little packets and taken to school for presents, or given to people whom we visited. It was always welcomed, for our friends and our neighbours did not waste good butter and good time in making sweets.

No shop sold coconuts, and we had to rely on the prowess of a farm man at a fair to knock off a coconut in the 'shy', for we could not dislodge the brown hairy nuts wedged tightly in iron rings.

Candied Flowers

Cowslips and narcissi, forget-me-nots and daisies can be candied for cake decoration. Three teaspoonfuls of gum-arabic in crystal form (this is important), is put in a bottle and covered with three tablespoonfuls of orange-flower water. Leave three days to dissolve, shaking often. Use a small paint brush, to cover the petals of the flowers, the calyx and the other parts, separately and carefully. Then dredge lightly with caster sugar and gently shake off the loose sugar. Dry in a hot cupboard on paper and store in a tin. The flowers must be freshly picked and must never be picked when wet. Care must be taken that edible flowers only are used. Violets, roses, and apple blossom and almond blossom are good flowers also, and heather may be used.

Hill Top Toffee

This is called 'an excellent toffee' by a countrywoman who made it. Three quarters of a pound of brown and white sugar mixed are boiled with two tablespoonfuls of black treacle, two ounces of butter, half a cup of milk and a little vinegar. Boil together until the toffee sets in cold water. Cut and wrap.

Molasses Candy

Two cups of sugar and half a cup of water, which must be boiling. Dissolve the sugar and add a quarter of a cup of vinegar and an ounce of butter. Boil together until a drop hardens in water.

Almond Hardbake

A pound of loaf sugar, and a teaspoonful of cream of tartar are boiled with half a pint of water, until golden. Then add a quarter of a pound of almonds and stir till they are also coloured golden. Then pour quickly into a greased tin.

Honey Toffee

Boil ten ounces of butter and four ounces of pure honey with a quarter of a pint of water. Boil to make soft ball when tested. Pour on to a greased tin. Then cut the toffee into small lumps with greased scissors and wrap in grease-proof paper. Good for colds.

There was one word which I particularly disliked, and it was wholesome. So many dull things were wholesome— rice pudding, porridge, tapioca, rue tea and camomile tea, but a wholesome sweet had a label which made it popular. We could eat and enjoy it. The following sweets were 'Wholesome goodies'.

Wholesome Sweets

Put a pound of brown sugar and two pints of water in a brass saucepan and bring to boiling point. Add two ounces of butter and two teaspoonfuls of essence of peppermint. Boil till the testing stage. Pour on a well-greased dish and leave to cool. When cool enough to handle take the mixture up and fold it together and pull it till it is light in colour and silky in texture. Then cut in small pieces and wrap each bit in paper twisted at the end.

Wholesome Sweets, a second recipe

Boil one pound of brown sugar with two tablespoonfuls of vinegar to the soft ball stage (when tested in cold water the syrup forms a ball which on removal will flatten). Take from the fire and cool. When luke-warm add a teaspoonful of vanilla essence and half a pound of chopped almonds, blanched. Heat until creamy and drop in small lumps on a greased dish. When cold put each into a paper case.

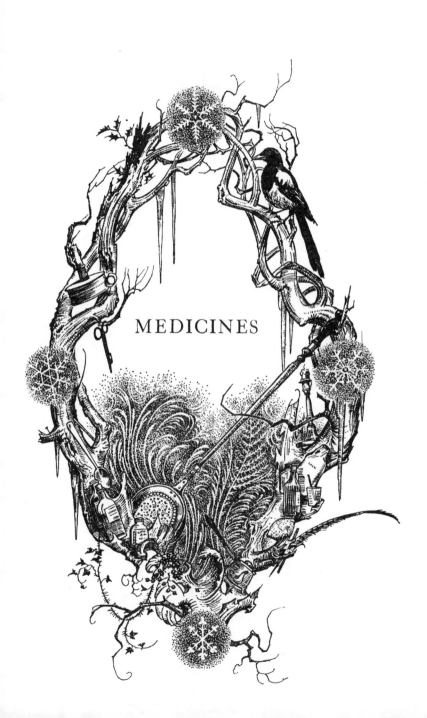

MEDICINES

LINIMENTS and ointments, cough mixtures and balms were made at home, and recipes for illnesses were passed on from one to another. The doctor lived miles away and as there was no telephone it meant a drive to fetch him when he would probably be a dozen miles away in the hills. So a man was despatched with a note and we awaited the answer.

The doctor came in his gig, driven by his groom, and our hill daunted even the doctor's mettlesome mare. Sometimes a bottle of medicine was left at one of the stone gateposts, on the wooded hillside, and there I ran to find the white parcel sealed with scarlet wax, neat and beautiful. I was much interested in any medicine and I liked the way bottles were wrapped and marked, and I was avid for a taste. But usually we made our own remedies.

One of the delicious remedies for a cold was raspberry vinegar. This old cure is still sold in the shops, and many older people buy it, I am told. In a letter from Moscow last year, a Russian writer told me that she got soaked to the skin in a storm, but she made a cup of raspberry tea, pouring boiling water on some raspberry leaves from her garden. She drank the infusion and went to bed. In the morning she had recovered, and she wished to know if we had the same remedy in our country. I was glad to say we had.

Raspberry Vinegar

Two quarts of white wine vinegar is poured over two quarts of fine freshly picked raspberries. Let it stand three or four days. Then strain and add a pound of sugar to each quart of liquid. Let it simmer to dissolve the sugar but do not boil. Bottle when cold. Take two teaspoonfuls for a cold.

Blackberry vinegar is made in a similar manner, and useful for a cold.

Raspberry Vinegar, a second recipe
(from an old Derbyshire farm)

Put two quarts of ripe raspberries into a jar with enough white wine vinegar to cover them. Let them stand for twenty-four hours. Put both fruit and vinegar into a pan and bring to the boil. Then strain, and to each pint of juice allow one pound of sugar. Put all into a pan and boil for twenty minutes, stirring well. When cold, bottle securely and store in a cool dry place.

Cough Cure, an old country recipe

Put into a saucepan a stick of liquorice, two ounces of fine linseed, two ounces of sugar candy, twenty-four raisins, and a pint and a half of water. Simmer all together with the lid on the pan. Strain and add the juice of a lemon. Bottle when cool. Take a tablespoonful every four hours.

Cough Mixture, well known in cottages

To a pint and a half of water add a pound of black treacle, two ounces of liquorice and boil for half an hour. Add a pennyworth of paregoric, a pennyworth of aniseed, and some oil of peppermint. When cold, bottle tightly. One tablespoonful every four hours.

Another Cough Mixture

The juice of three lemons is mixed with an equal quantity of salad oil, two pennyworth of paregoric and some honey to taste. Shake well before taking this cough mixture. Vinegar may be substituted for lemon juice if no lemons are available, but the flavour is not so nice.

Liniment

A drachm of oil of cloves and two drachms of amber, with nine drachms of camphorated oil. Mix together and rub on the chest or between the shoulders.

Recommended for lumbago were a little oil of juniper, from the berries, pounded, or a little bag of quicksilver kept in the pocket.

We ate delicious morsels of butter, honey and lemon juice, and home-made Everton toffee, when we had colds. We sipped blackcurrant tea and linseed tea, and we ate horehound toffee, a butterscotch flavoured with a few leaves of horehound from the garden. In the old days horehound was a herb in constant use for colds. A fire in the bedroom, sending shadows over the ceiling, a warming pan to heat the bed, and gruel to drink were further remedies. Then came reading aloud, when my mother sat in the wicker chair, which gave forth such squeaks in the dead of night that I was frightened. She would read a chapter of Masterman Ready or a tale of wolves in Russia and Canada, which made me shiver with delicious fright under my blankets.

Linseed Tea

This was a sovereign remedy for sore throats and colds. Half an ounce of linseed is washed and put in a saucepan with a pint of cold water. Simmer for half an hour. Add half an ounce of liquorice, and a quarter of an ounce of sugar candy. Strain and drink a little at a time.

Gruels, possets, teas and broths were made for the sick, and here are some recipes.

Egg Flip

This is an invalid drink. Beat up the yolk of an egg with a cup of milk. Then add a little port wine and a small amount of brandy. Sweeten to taste and add a sprinkle of nutmeg. It may be warmed, as a posset, but it must not be near boiling.

Treacle Posset

Warm a pint of milk, and pour into it a tablespoonful of black treacle. Boil for five minutes. Drink it hot. It is very good for a cough.

Chicken Broth

Cut up a good sized fowl into smallest pieces, the flesh and bones too. Put into a large earthenware jar or into a white lined pan with a lid, and cover with nearly a quart of water (cold). Let it simmer slowly after coming to the boil, for about three hours. When it has simmered for twenty minutes add a very little salt, some onion, parsley and celery to flavour it. By this simmering the whole must be reduced to not quite a pint. Strain through a fine hair sieve, and add salt to taste.

Beef Tea

One pound of lean buttock steak is cut in small pieces. Then pour half a pint (not more) of cold water on it. Add a pinch of salt and a small piece of Spanish onion. Cook very gently for three hours in a slow oven in a closed earthenware jar. Pour through a strainer and let it stand until cold. Skim off every small particle of fat that may be on it. When finished it should be deep rich brown in colour with the tiny particles of meat fibre suspended in it. No colouring matter or sauce of any kind to be added.

Dr. Broster's Lemon Water

Doctor Broster was a great character who lived about a hundred years ago. His fame endured and we heard many stories of his wit and sarcasm. He was all-powerful, and he knew how to deal with malingerers, but he was kind to the poor and helped everybody. He asked a great lady, 'How's your buels?', when she complained of sickness. His gig was the fastest, his household well-managed. He had servants and dogs and a fine house. When he died at a great age we bought his beautiful dinner service of early Staffordshire. His lemon water would be important.

To make a quart of lemon water. Cut the rind off two lemons. Add it to two tablespoonfuls of Demerara sugar. Pour a quart of boiling water over this. Add the juice of three lemons. It is ready for use, with or without a cold.

One can imagine the doctor growling 'Take it or leave it and be damned.'

The 'Three Oils', Amber, Cloves, and Camphorated, were used to rub chests, and the 'All Fours', Peppermint, Paregoric, Aniseed and Laudanum, were mixed together by the chemist, twopennyworth of each, to be diluted at home with treacle and water for cough mixtures.

SOME HERBS

I n our small herb garden we had plants of ancient lineage,
planted by my grandfather. Only my father knew the
names and he pointed out pennyroyal and horehound, peppermint and hyssop, tarragon, southernwood (lad's love to
us), basil, wormwood and rue. There was the little woodruff growing wild, and dill for babies, and mullein with its
tapering candles of flowers, and camomile which was like
a weed, aromatic and useful for our games.

In a little croft grew many flowers of purple mallow and
rose mallow, whose seeds I called 'green cheeses'. Once on
a time the mallow had been treasured for its healing properties, I was told, so it was never uprooted. Marjoram was
used in salads, and marjoram tea was made in the usual
way, by picking a few tips of the plants, infusing in boiling
water, and drinking a cupful.

I tasted the leaves of many a herb as I sat on the garden
seat safe from observation with my books and doll, and the
sage leaves tickled my legs with their green soft fingers; it
was a little tree in shape, sturdy and thickset, and I picked
the leaves for the kitchen, to make sage and onion dressing
when we had roast pork. There was wormwood which I
admired for its tassels of grey flowers, and for the legend

that anyone putting mugwort or wormwood in the shoe would never feel tired. I put some in my slipper and I was not tired, so it must be true!

I picked bunches of mint from the leaves which grew in thick green spires, scenting the air and refreshing everyone who stood near it. Peppermint was fragrant and delicate and strong, and a sprig went into boiling sugar when sweets were made. We never cut mint with a knife, but pulled it, or stripped the leaves. A drink was made with equal quantities of mint, pennyroyal and balm, sweetened with sugar.

Peppermint tea was used for indigestion and for a cold, and again one only poured boiling water on the leaves and the medicine was ready.

Mint was chopped finely and put in cream cheese to make a mint cheese, and it was used in butter to make mint-butter, for meat sandwiches. It was a flavouring for salads, and for a junket, one of the most useful herbs.

We always had a thick border of parsley along one of the garden paths, and parsley was used for parsley sauce, which was a creamy thick sauce with plenty of the finely chopped parsley so that it was green. It was used in cheese, to make a green layer, especially in cream cheese.

Sage was the colouring for Christmas cheese, when three or four bands of green were visible in the creamy cheese we had each year at Christmas. Sage was a herb of tradition, and when I sat on the garden seat, hidden from sight, I watched the bees enter the purple flowers of the sage and I picked the grey leaves and held them squeezed in my hands to get the oil and the scent.

A bunch of sage hung from the kitchen ceiling, where it kept flies from the room and made a good odour. Rosemary too was a herb to hang up in a room, or to put among the blankets of the chest, or the sheets in the second oak chest.

Sage tea was made for a cold, an ounce of leaves to a pint of boiling water, and the liquid drunk like tea, not treated as a medicine. Also it was used as a gargle for a sore throat, when a little honey was added and the brew was made stronger.

Woodruff, lavender, rosemary and dried rose petals were used for the oak chests where linen and blankets were stored. There was always a delicious odour when I lifted the heavy lids to take out a towel or a treasure hidden there. Dried thyme, and dried rosemary branches, made a good deterrent to moths, and we added a few cloves for extra. We gathered wild thyme from a valley whose steep banks were littered with stones among which the wild thyme flourished.

Rue tea, from the garden herb, was made in spring as a bitter brew which was good for us. I had to drink my share. I tasted a leaf from the ferny tree, but the bitterness was so strong I could not understand why some old people actually ate sandwiches of rue for tea.

The little herb garden was a source of intimate pleasure, and although I did not care for the taste of herbs, I got to know them very well. I breathed in their strange scents, and gazed at the shapes of their leaves and flowers, as I sat alone with bees and ants and hover flies in the hot sunshine.

Index

The names of recipes are in italics